This book is dedicated
to my best friend, help mate, intercessor,
encourager, prayer-partner, and sweetheart . . .
my precious wife, Cheri.

ISBN 1-931600-72-4

Scriptures from the New King James Version

Family Ministries, Inc.
Lake Junaluska, NC USA
www.familyministries.net

Printed by Faith Printing in the United States of America

CONTENTS

INTRODUCTION

What does any twenty-one year old really know about marriage? Scott thought he was ready for marriage. After all, he was a college student with above-average intelligence, had parents who were happily married, and had been analyzing marriages and relationships for some time. He was fairly well-adjusted, had self-control and was absolutely, positively, head-over-heels in love with Cheri. In their whirlwind, one year, long distance courtship, they never had a fight, not even a heated discussion. They agreed on most of the major issues. They were married August 14th, 1971. Then the work began. God began to melt, mold, shape and teach them His plan for their marriage.

In his own uniquely candid style, Scott begins each chapter of this book with a reflection of his thoughts as he stood before the altar on his wedding day, saying his marriage vows. Then, based on over twenty-eight years of marital experience, he shares some of the circumstances which have tested the depth of his commitment to those vows. His conversations with God thread their way throughout the narrative as the circumstances that challenged his vows gave opportunity for him to grow in the understanding of true commitment and love.

Will you, Scott, take Cheri
To be your lawfully
wedded wife,
To have and to hold,
In sickness and health,
For richer for poorer,
Forsaking all others,
As long as you both shall live?
If so answer, I do.

Chapter 1

Do you, Scott, take Cheri to be your lawfully wedded wife?

As a young man I had so many hopes and dreams, most of which centered around me and what I wanted. These included a beautiful wife who would support and compliment me on the road towards my lofty goals. Looking back I now realize how self-centered most young people are . . . at least it seemed I was that way.

For example, as I think back on my wedding vows, I can clearly see how my expectations were basically those of a 'user' relationship. Little did I realize then how my commitment to the vows I would make that day would be tested through the years.

I remember that I was almost in a daze, mesmerized by my radiant bride as the Pastor spoke our vows . . .

Will I take her? You bet I will . . . and never let her go! This long distance courtship is tiring. Those weekend cannonball runs to see her are over. This evening when I say goodnight I won't be hanging up the phone or getting in the car by myself and driving home. All those things we've dreamed of! It seems funny -- last night God wouldn't approve of the intimacy we now are expected to share. I love her so much; I can't wait to be alone with her. My wedded wife. I like the sound of that. Someone to meet my every need . . . a clean house, clean clothes, three square meals a day, children and lots of love. I'm really going to like this!

~~~

Perhaps your background is similar to mine, perhaps not. What's important is how I applied what I learned growing up to my marriage. You see, I was raised by a mother who was absolutely incredible. She had eight children and kept us clean, fed, and happy. When I think of Mom I always remember her as having on an apron. The kitchen was her domain. I still crave some of her special dishes. Mom always played a supportive role to Dad. He worked and brought in the paycheck. She took care of the home, the kids, and Dad's needs. Dad was definitely the head, but Mom was the heartbeat. Mom was extremely intelligent, but she never went to college. She could have been anything she wanted to be, but she was content with her role as a mother. I can't imagine her ever giving a thought to being anything other than what she was: a mother, a homemaker, and Dad's support. When I was dating I would often shmooze up to my mom with a chorus of "I want a girl just like the girl that married dear old Dad."
~~~

Cheri took possession of my heart and emotions the first time I saw her picture. My match-making grandmother had sent me a newspaper clipping of the recently crowned county beauty queen who attended her church. She was a beautiful, talented Christian girl from a prominent family in her church, and my grandma knew her well. This was too good to be true. My Grandma Marie loved me and was promoting this girl. I saw a definite opportunity here. So I wrote her and to my surprise she wrote back. It was love at first 'write'. She was an honor student who loved music, was a terrific singer, traveled with her college choir, and attended college in my home state. She displayed a confidence and poise that said "I can be whatever I want to be." I was a visionary who was going to save the world. Here was a girl who could stand by my side and help me realize all my dreams and aspirations. She was intelligent, talented, ambitious and beautiful.

~~~

About eight years after our wedding came a time of testing. I can clearly remember how I felt as we went through some pretty trying times at the retreat center that we owned and operated . . .

I wonder how much she can take. She has always been so strong. Any counselor would say she is showing signs of an impending nervous breakdown. Life had been going along so smoothly; so how did we
~~~

get in this predicament? Her radical diet really has me worried. She's lost over twenty pounds, and I never thought she was heavy in the first place. She's way too thin, but she won't listen to me. Why should she? I put the pressure on her to sell our cute little cottage on the lake and buy this retreat center. It seemed like such an honorable effort. "We have a call on our lives for ministry, honey," I told her. "This is God's will for us." So we bought the retreat center in an effort to help heal wounded marriages. Now ours is ending up in a mess. We both are emotionally, spiritually, and financially drained. No matter how optimistic I am, the fact is we're falling behind on our payments. It's only a matter of time before we're going to lose it all. The group home seemed like such a good idea. Taking in troubled teenage boys seemed like a win-win situation. We could help some troubled teen-age delinquent boys by ministering the love of Jesus in a solid Christian family environment while the state paid us to do so. Cheri has been taking care of our three kids, the eight foster boys, and has been doing all the laundry and cleaning at the retreat center. It's been like holding down three full-time jobs and definitely has taken its toll on her. She's been threatened repeatedly by the boys. Last week one grabbed a two-by-four and took a swing at her. She almost packed up the kids and left that day. I never thought she could leave me, but I know she was fearful for the kids as well as herself.

There were many incidents with the foster boys that would have made most women call it quits. Cheri really was quite a perfectionist, and trying to balance all her responsibilities at the retreat center stretched her beyond what most women could endure. I couldn't believe it when she announced she was going to start her own business selling Mary Kay Cosmetics. Knowing everything else we were dealing with, I couldn't imagine how she could get involved with this. I knew it wouldn't do any good to protest, and I couldn't disagree with the fact that we needed the money. She went to the bank and got a loan so that she could have her products on hand. I shook my head in disbelief that she could convince a bank officer to give her a $2,000 loan. But one of the reasons I liked her from the start was that confidence she displayed. Her little business proved to be absolutely incredible! In just a short period of time she had risen to a top level position and was making a great deal of money. She had changed from a wilted flower into a blossoming rose. It's as if a miracle had taken place.

~~~

Thinking back on what a blessing Cheri's business was for us, it seems ironic that I had such a struggle with it at that time. It was really hard on me, mostly because of my own pride. She managed to handle all her responsibilities at the retreat center, including the care
~~~

of the foster boys, even better than before. She didn't neglect me or our kids; in fact she took the kids with her when she attended conferences where they would have fun, supervised activities. As I vacillated from anger to depression over her "business" I knew I had to get on my knees and talk it over with God . . .

God, what is wrong with me? After years of serving me, caring for the kids, supporting my ministry and doing whatever else I pushed on her, she is doing something ***she*** *wants to do. She's so motivated and excited; Mary Kay seems to have brought fulfillment into her life in a way I never could. God, I'm struggling here! I'm frustrated with the fact that she's making more money than I am. I'm straining at attending those stupid conventions. And I'm sick and tired of being introduced as 'Cheri Scheer's husband'. I need some major help here!*

When God speaks to me He usually gets right to the point. I suppose if He didn't I would be off dreaming about some new adventure, never waiting for His reply. But I sure couldn't miss Him this time . . .

You're not going to like what I have to say, but then you usually don't. First, you're still in bondage to that "keep her barefoot, pregnant, and in the kitchen" macho garbage. You want to be the big cheese, the big man in control. As long as ***she*** *makes* ***you*** *look good and fulfills* ***your*** *needs, you're happy. This is* ***her*** *hour; you need to support her in this. So tell me,* *what makes you think that your self-centered direction of her life has been such a blessing? It's amazing that she's been able to break out of the cage you've had her in and regain her confidence to try something that wasn't your idea. Your wife is not a cook, housekeeper, laundress, sex object and baby-maker. She is My precious daughter given to you by Me to help make you complete. Her opinion counts. Her desires should be of major concern to you. She is much more sensitive, level-headed, patient and discerning than you'll ever be. You were meant to be a team. You're not the coach and she the water-girl. There was a time when you were* ***attracted*** *to her abilities. Now that she's receiving some recognition, you're jealous. In an effort to distract attention from your own low self-image you have tried to keep her down. That won't help you feel better about yourself. It will only make things worse. You wouldn't be in the mess you're in if you had listened to your wife in the first place.*

That hurt, but I knew it was the truth. Cheri had not felt peace about buying the retreat center in the first place. But, it was one of those 'I'm right, I'm the man' issues. I hated to be reminded of that. But God wasn't through with me yet. He went on to rebuke me with the same Scripture I had quoted so many times when counseling other men . . .

Remember, Scott, you and Cheri are one. You're not in competition. ***Her*** *victories are* ***your*** *victories. You'll find fulfillment by meeting her needs and encouraging her. "Husbands love your wives even as Christ loved the church and gave himself for it" is as true for you as any other man.*

Those words pierced deep into my aching heart. I realized at that time, however, that I had a choice to make. Either I obeyed God and changed my mind about the role my wife would have in my life, or our situation would stay the same . . . and most likely even get worse .

~~~

God had taught us both a new meaning for the term 'wife'. A husband needs to recognize his wife as the one who stands beside him. She is his partner. As with any partnership, the opinions, feelings and strengths of both parties are valuable to the relationship. A wife is not there to do everything the husband doesn't want to do. She is there to support him, working with him to fulfill their mutual dreams. Partners should edify, not criticize one another. Their strengths should compliment each other so that they are better together than they are separately.

A woman needs to view her role as a wife as one of honor. She is entrusted with the position of being the
~~~

perfect helper for her husband. God holds her husband responsible for their welfare and simply asks her to love and support him as the head of their home.

Ultimately we did leave the retreat center and moved on to a new ministry. Praise God for Cheri's hard work and sacrifice during those years. The money saw us through a tough time when we lost the retreat center and paid creditors. After a few years, the Lord told Cheri that she should resign from Mary Kay. She gave up her business and waved goodbye to the pink car, prizes, success, recognition and big paychecks. She felt that God had released her to support me full-time in the ministry once again. She had changed. Once again her direction and focus on ministry was from her heart. And she didn't mind being introduced as "Pastor Scott's wife".

MISS MUSKEGON COUNTY

Chapter 2

To have and to hold

To have forever. She's all mine and no one else's. She belongs to me, even takes my name: "Mrs. Scott Scheer". Yeah, I really like the sound of that. What does 'have' really mean anyway? To own, control, take for my own, possess, hold captive? I can see it in her eyes, she wants to have me as much as I want to have her. We want to have each other, possess each other, captivate one another for all eternity. I will never leave her side. I'll keep her so close that I can have her and hold her whenever I want. I'll never forget the first time I held her. It was at that crazy drive-in movie "Herbie Goes to Monte Carlo". Holding her for the first time was so exciting. Sometimes I hold her so tight I'm afraid that I'm going to break her ribs. "To have and to hold", no problem with that vow. I'm going to hold her so close people will think we're Siamese twins! Holding her has become my favorite pastime. To touch her, to feel the warmth of her body, to smell her hair. How am I ever going to work all day without her by my side?

~~~

It's hard to believe that only five years later Cheri wanted us to get some marriage counseling. The thought of going to a counselor for help with our mar-
~~~

riage had never entered my mind. Perhaps it was because my pride had blocked it out. No counselor was going to analyze me. I didn't need counseling. . . it was Cheri who had all the problems. I'm sure my stern demeanor was very intimidating as we sat in Pastor Bob's office, but rather than whole-heartedly listening, I was inwardly murmuring about being there.

***We** don't need counseling, we **do** counseling. Sure we have our differences and we don't always see eye-to-eye, but counseling? We are opposites, but we don't get violent or verbally abusive. Maybe counseling **would** be a good thing. I think she might listen to a counselor and finally see that I'm not the only one who thinks she has problems. That's it! Why should I fight the idea? This is my big chance to get her straightened out! She wants to see Pastor Bob; that's a good idea. He's sure to see my point of view. After all, we're both men in ministry.*

Can you believe that?! She told him that she doesn't feel the same love for me that she once did. She feels our love is tired. That's great! After all I've sacrificed for her. I work so hard to give her a good life; she ought to be falling all over me. I'll drop anything to give her some attention. I try to touch her but she can't be bothered -- she's changing a diaper. Try to give her a little loving, and all I get is rejection; she has to get supper going. We go to bed and she says she's so tired that she just wants to go to sleep. ***I'm*** *the one who goes to work all day! All she has to do is stay home and take care of three little kids. She gets out to the grocery store and goes shopping whenever she wants. If anyone should be falling out of love it should be me!*

What a disappointment this has turned out to be! Pastor Bob wants us to come back next week and take a temperament test. Well, he's right about one thing; she sure does have a temper! We don't need a test to see that.

~~~

I couldn't believe I actually found myself back in Pastor Bob's office one week later. We had taken the temperament tests and I was sure it would reveal that Cheri had some real problems. She was very interested as he began to explain the results but I was preoccupied with my own thoughts . . .

Okay Bob, the test was clever. So I'm a high 'I' (influence) personality. Oh this is deep. I could have told you that my temperament type desires social recognition, popularity, people to talk with, freedom from control and freedom from details. What do you mean 'this type of person is easily distracted from tasks, and fears loss of recognition'? So what? Okay, I guess it nailed me; that's definitely me. But, I think that's the way everyone should be -- people first.
~~~

Okay, Cheri, it's your turn. Maybe the truth will come out. Yeah, I knew it. She's a high 'D' (dominance): quick to take action, creates change, takes charge, gets results, authoritative, direct, a decisive decision-maker, challenges power and authority, fears being taken advantage of -- that's my baby alright! The problem seems quite clear to me.

Come on, Bob. What do you mean there is no wrong or right, we're just different?!

~~~

I really don't know why I was so surprised at what Pastor Bob told us. He explained that there are four basic temperament groups but as many variations as there are people. Society works because everyone is different. If we were all leaders, who would follow? If everyone was a speaker, who would listen? Marriage works when each partner realizes that his way of thinking which may seem right for him, could be quite different from that of his spouse. They may approach the same situation in different ways. One basic reason opposites attract is that often one person admires the qualities in another person that he doesn't possess himself. Another reason is God knows what will make the best combination, the best <u>team</u>.

I had to admit that made a lot of sense. I paid better attention as Pastor Bob explained why Cheri responded to me the way she did when she was busy with something . . .
~~~

*So you're saying that she needs to **feel** that she is at a point of completion, whether she's finished or not, before she goes on to something else? In other words, she isn't rejecting me when I try to take her away from a task and she doesn't give me attention right then. It's not easy to admit that her response isn't wrong -- just different than mine would be. I guess it's just her God-given makeup to finish the task she's started before starting a new one, even if that 'task' is me. Maybe if I would help her finish what she's doing she would be more receptive to my affection.*

~~~

It was a humbling experience to realize that I might be wrong about two things: 1) I did need counseling and 2) the problems we were having in our relationship weren't all my wife's fault. I was contemplating the need for a little repentance so I opened my heart to God . . .

Lord, is that what You meant when You said, "husbands, dwell with them according to knowledge, giving honor unto thy wife"? You made them different for a purpose, didn't you?

As I began to think about all the wonderful differences between Cheri and myself, I'm sure it was the Holy Spirit who reminded me of the attributes I saw in her when we first met. I loved those things that were uniquely hers; like the wonderful way she could organize anything, and how about the way she would
~~~

stick with even the most mundane task until it was done . . . and done well! All of her dumb little 'things to do' lists were blessings in disguise. She got more projects finished than I ever thought of starting. I found myself feeling a little sheepish as I remained in the presence of my God who could see right through me. He so graciously ministered to my heart as He continued . . .

Before the foundations of the world I knew you and Cheri. As a teenager you would pray for a perfect woman to become your wife. Don't you believe that I answered your prayer when you met Cheri? I brought her to you as a gift. Even though neither one of you is perfect, you are a perfect match. Together your giftings and abilities make a better whole. You have wasted so much energy trying to change her. My perfect plan is for your differences to compliment each other. Your visionary gift has brought great purpose into your lives; her organizational skills have helped you complete the things you've dreamed of. So often you struggle with her emotional make-up. Even ***those*** *differences help complete you as a man.*

~~~

"To have and to hold" has taken on a brand new meaning in our marriage. To 'have' his wife a husband needs to submit himself to God's authority. When he follows God's direction, his wife can be secure in his
~~~

leadership, trusting him with the welfare of the family. He 'holds' his wife by respecting her as an equal partner in their marriage. As they seek God together for guidance in every situation she will feel confident that her husband values her as his help mate. Rather than 'being in control', he is to lead under God's authority and direction. He demonstrates his willingness to 'have' her as he lovingly protects and honors her as a gift from God.

A wife 'holds' her husband by following his direction when he includes her in seeking God for guidance. With the security that she can rely on him to fulfill his role as the spiritual head of the family she shows that she respects his authority and holds him in a position of trust. By supporting her husband in his leadership role within the family, a wife demonstrates her confidence in her husband's desire to hear and obey the Lord's voice. When the husband submits to God's authority and his wife in turn submits herself to her husband she shows that she will 'have' him as her husband.

Over the years, Cheri and I have learned to appreciate our differences. We have encouraged each other in our weak areas and capitalized on our strengths. We have found that by submitting ourselves to the Lord and to each other, God's design in making us a team becomes increasingly clear.

Chapter 3

In sickness and in health

Well, this should be an easy one. Just by looking at Cheri anyone can see that she's in great health. She exercises, seems to eat right, and stays in terrific shape. Oh that terrific shape. From where I'm standing there is nothing wrong with this girl! Of course, I know heredity has a lot to do with health. Her mother seems very healthy. I don't ever remember Cheri saying anything about her being sick or having any surgery. Then there are her grandmothers. Both are living to a ripe old age and they seem in good health. Good health and long life seem to run in her family. This vow ought to be a synch to keep; she comes from good genes. I shouldn't have to worry about the 'in sickness and in health' part. Of course, her dad died at thirty-nine. He had some kind of heart problem, but I think it was related to a surgery or something in the hospital. I hate hospitals. I sure hope neither of us ever have to go to the hospital. I couldn't stand seeing her sick.

~~~

Twenty-five years later I had the opportunity to test those feelings. I was in the office at church when Cheri came in and said she needed to talk to me. She had been part of a study for some new medication and
~~~

in the process went through some intensive tests. When the results came back, there was something that didn't look quite right. She was going to the doctor for more tests to determine if there was anything seriously wrong. The suffering I experienced as Cheri calmly endured test after test was unbearable. I can remember my feeling of helplessness as the doctor explained that she would need surgery. I was almost a basket-case the day I checked her in to the hospital . . .

How could this have happened? She's only in her mid-forties. She feels fine and looks great. Without those stupid tests we never would have known anything was wrong. She eats right and exercises regularly. Now she needs surgery? The doctors said one hour for pre-op, two hours for surgery, and an hour for recovery . . . if all goes well. What did they mean by that -- if?

I can't believe I'm sitting in a hospital waiting room while my wife is being operated on. I never thought either of us would be in the hospital . . . this just isn't a part of my plan. I would much rather be out fishing right now. What am I saying? I promised to love her in sickness as well as in health. My place is with her, or as close as I can get.

As I sat in the waiting room a nurse came with some paper work that I had to fill out. I was sure she could see how nervous I was and probably just wanted to keep me busy. Every time the surgical door opened I took a deep breath and hoped it would be her doctor saying everything went fine. The time seemed to drag on and on and my imagination went into hyper-speed.

I wonder what's going on in that operating room right now? She's always been so healthy except for a little sinus problem now and then. A vision of strength, able to do the work of two women, she has seemingly boundless energy. She has her 'things to do list' that never seems to end. She's always been too busy to get sick. God has been so faithful at keeping her healthy. I have always been so dependent on her great energy and ability to get a job done. I've down-right taken her for granted. She's worked way too hard over the years -- raising three kids, teaching school, helping in the ministry, and keeping the house. I put way too much on her. It's **my** *fault she's having surgery! I expect so much out of her; I push her too hard. I wish I could relive these years. I definitely would do it differently. My own selfishness put her under so much pressure and stress. I'm so demanding and I know it. 'Mr. Selfish! Serve me, help me, meet my needs.' That's probably why she's developed these problems and is having surgery today. I'm the one who should be in there experiencing all the pain and trauma!*

The few times that Cheri had been sick almost paralyzed our household. Life in the Scheer house as we had come to know it came to a halt. As I look back

I wondered, "in those moments when I prayed for her to be healed, was it for her sake, or mine?" I couldn't believe how my thoughts were consumed with concern for her . . .

I wonder if she's out from being under anesthesia yet? I sure hope she didn't have to wait long in the holding area. Her back always bothers her if she lays flat too long.

Like sheep being led to the slaughter I found myself saying, "Yes Doctor, whatever you say Doctor". I felt so out of control. This third-party-doctor-person was calling all the shots. I don't like it when I'm not the one who is in control. Still, I've found that it's much better to leave things in God's hands, let Him be the one in control. So I turned to God with all my fears and worry . . .

God, You put Cheri in my trust. You've instructed me to protect, provide, and love her. There isn't much I can do in this waiting room while they do who-knows-what in the operating room. You know God, I really love this girl and I'm really concerned about her.

I really felt immobilized as I sat with my head bowed on folded hands. It wasn't despair, but a wondering what God's will was in all this. I didn't wait long for His reply . . .

I love her, too, and I loved her first. I have also loved her longer, and I love her much more because I have more love to give.

Before I even seemed to think: *"But God, she's my wife! What would I do without her?"* He responded to me with, *"But she's **MY** daughter."*

All of the sudden it hit me. Cheri was in much better hands than mine. God was taking care of her. He was in the operating room with her. She was His daughter.

~~~

When I contemplate how much God loves Cheri as His daughter, I can't help but compare it to how much I love my own daughters. When they were growing up I would have done anything to make them happy. Cheri and I prayed for their husbands since the day they were conceived. When Jarred and Ray came along, they sort of waltzed right in and took my daughters away from me. I was convinced that there was no way they could ever care for them as well I had. I had been willing to make any sacrifice for their well-being and I still would. Of course they're wonderful husbands and both of them fully understand their responsibility to take care of their wives. Still I do check up on my girls all the time. Even though they're married, I'll always be their father.

~~~

So my beloved wife was God's daughter first. He has unlimited love and resources to meet her needs. Technically, I'm part of God's plan to meet those needs. Now *that's* a sobering thought. I had been granted the privilege of being a minister of God's love and grace to one of His special daughters. When I became selfish or demanded my own way, I failed my assignment. I hate to think how many times I have failed. While she was in surgery I couldn't protect or comfort her. That's when I had to trust her Heavenly Father to do the job alone. With this realization I was able to find the peace that God promises us.

In the midst of this trial were some of the best weeks of our entire marriage. God used the experience to give me an advanced degree in 'husbandhood'. He taught me that when my wife has a need, nothing else matters. My love for God and my commitment to Him is manifested by the love I show to my wife. It's God first, wife second. Romans eight verse twenty-eight sure has applied to our marriage. "For all things work together for good for those who love God and are called according to His purpose." His main purpose for me is to take care of His little girl. I took her to her nine doctor's appointments. I sat with her in the waiting rooms. I held her hand during testing, met with doctors, and helped track down test results. I gathered reading material related to her problem and we both became informed. Sharing an understanding of what she was going through, and praying with her for God's wisdom, strength and healing was the support she needed. I did it with joy knowing that it was a blessing to her and pleasing to God.

~~~

This experience has enhanced our marriage. Our morning devotion times have become incredible. It became so much easier to pray and read the Word together, sensing a need to press in. As I sought the Lord on how I could better minister to Cheri, He gave me some incredible direction. Every morning I would give her a massage and pray over her. For the first time in our marriage I felt like I was literally *covering* her with prayer. As I gave her a massage, I prayed over every joint and muscle group saying, "bless these discs and vertebrae, bless her cardiovascular system. Lord, let every organ perform according to Your creative plan. Renew her mind and take control of her nervous system. Balance her sugar levels, her red and white blood cells. Let her glands and body chemistry work in perfect harmony." I bound, I loosed, I prayed protection and God's blessings. The result was that we changed and so did our marriage. I thanked God for the entire experience. What we gained far outweighed what we went through.

~~~

Cheri came through the surgery just fine. The hospital let me stay by her side through her entire stay. I helped whenever I could. I rubbed her back, arranged her flowers and talked about the things we would do together once she was well. Most of the time she just rested and I held her hand and prayed. Within a few weeks, she was back to normal. I had functioned quite well in health, and now had learned about being a faithful husband during sickness. I wasn't in control, but I knew who was and I trusted Him.

Chickering Photo

Chapter 4

For richer, for poorer

Who needs money? We can live on love! Money's no big deal. We both knew how to make do with very little. One thing about being part of a big family is you learn how to work. I was mowing lawns or shoveling walks and manure by age ten. Dad taught us how to make it on our own. He told me that I couldn't drive his car after I turned sixteen. I would either have to buy my own car or walk. He helped me set up a savings account at the bank and out of every paycheck I put money aside for my car. I worked my way through college. I was a full-time student, had a full-time job and still had fun. Cheri started working right after her father died and she hasn't stopped since. She is so ambitious, I expect that by the time we're in our forties, we'll be millionaires. 'For richer, for poorer', not a worry!

~~~

Just a few years after I made this vow I learned its real meaning through the school of experience. I was going down for the third time and my thoughts betrayed the funnel of financial frustration we were in . . .
~~~

I don't know how much longer we can make it! We're two months behind on our farm payment. The feed bill keeps getting bigger and the milk checks keep getting smaller. They won't extend anymore credit at the feed store. No matter how many times I go over the figures, they keep coming out the same. The payment on the cows, their feed and all the expenses are greater than our income. I just ***love*** *the privilege of milking those cows every morning and every evening, cleaning the gutters, putting down bedding, and feeding and watering them -- just to lose money. I have a tractor payment on a tractor that won't run. I feel awful telling the creditors they should have already received their payment. In all honesty, they should have received payment - but I had not sent the checks out yet. I would like to send out the checks, but if I did they would bounce to the moon. "Life on the farm is kind'a laid back . . ." Not on this farm! I milked the cows at five this morning, taught school all day, came home, did the chores and milked the cows again. Here I am at eleven at night with a flashlight, picking up the ears of corn that the old picker missed. For what?! To make a few more bucks to get some creditor off my back for another month? And then what? It's a vicious circle.*

At least work had kept me out of the house. I got so tired of listening to, "I told you not to buy the farm. If you would have listened to me we wouldn't be in this mess. I slave away all day taking care of these kids, changing diapers, making your meals, putting up canned goods, and feeding those stupid chickens. Then there are those cows. I told you not to buy those cows." I was in a place where I didn't know what to do. Unfortunately, when men get to a place like that they usually take out their frustration on their wives.

I wondered if Cheri thought I liked working around the clock while getting further behind. I didn't appreciate the 'I told you so' jabs. She never quite remembered things the way I did. It had been our dream to have a farm, raise a family and live happily ever after. It sure was a whole lot easier before we had the kids, when we were both working. We used to laugh so much. We used to have time for friends and each other. Now it seemed like every time we were together, all we did was fight about finances. There was so much excitement when we first moved to the farm and fixed up the house. I'll never forget the day I bought Cheri a horse for her birthday. She was so surprised. I never thought I'd hate the farm **or** our life. I didn't really blame God for our situation, but there was so much frustration within me . . .

Lord, it's that woman you gave me; she's always on my back; she never lets up reminding me of our bills. I can't work any harder than I already am . . .

As I wallowed in my self-pity I was amazed to hear God speak . . .

Why don't you quit your complaining and listen to Me for a change? Your problem is you won't listen . . . to Me ***or*** *your wife.*

I couldn't believe God said that! I was already feeling defeated. I thought that what I needed was some comfort, not rebuke. After all, I had spent lots of time talking to God, and I was quick to remind Him of that.

Now God that's just not fair. I talk to You while I milk the cows. I talk to You for hours while I'm riding the tractor. I'm up early in the morning and late at night with no one else to talk to but You!

God didn't give me much time to complain. He was quick to point out that He was aware of the fact that I was talking **to** Him. That was just the point . . .

But Scott, ***you*** *do all the talking. You never listen to what* ***I*** *have to say. You do the same thing with Cheri. You think you're open to her input, but you don't listen to her. You don't consider her feelings. You don't value her opinion. If you feel she doesn't agree with you, you manipulate her into tears. If she raises her voice at all, or seems at all critical of your ideas, you shut her out.*

Scott, you think Cheri is manipulating you but you are deceived. Her over-reacting comes out of her frustra-

tion. She feels it's the only way she can get through to you. So often you start out your conversations by saying, "I know you're not going to be in favor of this, but . . ." Then you proceed to play your mind-game of "I wonder where we'd be if you didn't always say no or shoot down my ideas." I'll tell you where you would be, in a lot better place than you are right now! Your inability to listen to Me and find that place of agreement with your wife has taken you out of My perfect plan for you. Cheri was given to you as a compliment. You are an impulsive risk-taker. Cheri is steady, calculated, level-headed and cautious. She's not always right, but she **is** *your balance. The sooner you realize this, the easier life will be for you.*

~~~

I realized that God had told me exactly what I needed to hear. And I had a good idea of what I needed to do about our present situation. I knew if I would admit my fault and ask Cheri to forgive me we could go to God together and ask for His help.

As I shared my intent to really listen to her ideas, Cheri began to soften. She could hear my heart and became very compassionate towards the frustration I was feeling. I knew we were moving towards agreement.

Together we sought the Lord's face, asked forgiveness and thanked Him for direction and financial deliverance.
~~~

We followed God's guidance as He instructed us to sell the farm -- lock, stock and dairy herd. The Lord then opened a new door and we moved to Maryland where we worked in a youth ministry. We learned how to listen more closely to God and each other. We found that when we came into a place of agreement things worked out best. When I would bully my way, we always encountered opposition. Within four years we owned a modest cottage (which we used as an office/home) and a motor home. We began traveling, doing evangelism ministry. Best of all, we had almost totally eliminated fights over finances.

Chapter 5

Forsaking all others

"I want to be loved by you, by you, and nobody else but you . . . want to be loved by you alone." That song says it all. My wandering days are over. I've prayed for God to bring me the right woman and I know Cheri's the one. Sure, I enjoyed dating. I had lots of fun. I enjoyed the variety of different personalities. Actually, dating was a pain. It was a hunt for the right woman, filled with pressure and stress, trying to impress each girl. Can you imagine what it would be like if you married a girl that you continuously had to impress day after day?! Everything with Cheri is so natural. I can really be myself. My search for the right woman is over; I have found her. I just can't imagine being unfaithful. You find the right one, and that's that. Well, one thing for sure, I don't have to worry about Cheri and she certainly doesn't have to worry about me. 'Hound-dog' is my middle name.

~~~

Just fifteen years later, as I enjoyed another beautiful Florida day, I became sensitized to the full meaning of the vow "forsaking all others". It was a perfect day for running. The temperature was around eighty degrees
~~~

with only a slight breeze, and the tide was low, leaving a wide, flat sandy beach. Running on the beach was an ultimate high for me. I loved those short escapes from the office monotony. There was nothing like having the sun on my back and a gentle ocean breeze to keep me cool. When we lived up north, my running was seasonal. I was always interrupted by the cold and snow of winter. Living in Florida and being able to run all year round was really a blessing. I felt that I was in the best shape I'd been in for years. The best part about my "run" time was that I used it as a prayer time with the Lord. Four miles each way gave me a good hour to pray. It seemed like I could pray better when I ran. No one was there to bother me -- just a few sea birds. The old legs felt pretty good that day, and I thought I might be able to run for ten miles. Then I was suddenly distracted. Walking in front of me was a well-shaped girl who looked quite bare. As I got closer I could see that she was wearing one of those 'thong' type suits. The moment of decision was upon me. I slowed my pace and struggled with my thoughts. Should I turn back, run by her without looking, witness to her, or could I get away with enjoying the 'view'? Wouldn't you know, she turned around and looked right at me with a great big smile. It was almost as if she was inviting me to run up beside her and start talking. I was surprised by my thoughts . . . I felt flattered! Suddenly, I saw myself as a pretty good looking, middle-aged man in good shape who looked attractive to this young woman. I kept running, feeling quite guilty, and started rationalizing the whole experience to God . . .

So what's the big deal, God?! So I looked. She looked at me first. And I felt a little flattered. She's a very attractive girl and <u>*she*</u> *noticed me. Cheri doesn't make a fuss over my physique like she should. I run and work out to keep in good shape for her and she acts like she could care less. After all, I don't want a relationship with that girl; I just took a look. You're the one who made the female body so desirable to look at, and you made men want to look. It's more like appreciating fine art or a beautiful animal. There's no invasion of privacy here. She's out on a public beach for all to see.*

I knew what God would say to that. I said it to myself. "Am I trying to reason with you, God, or justify my sin. I was tempted. I gave in." Just as I was thinking maybe I should quit running on the beach I heard God.

Running on the beach is ***not*** *the problem. Location has nothing to do with what just happened. It's not* ***where*** *you are but* ***who*** *you are. You just had an encounter with lust. Men everywhere struggle with it. Once you noticed her you didn't have to entertain thoughts about her; you didn't have to keep looking! Having a young, attractive woman smile at you shouldn't bring up feelings of discontent with the way your wife treats you.*

I started thinking about the way I felt when I saw men stare at my daughters. I had no idea if they were having sexual thoughts towards my girls, but I knew I didn't like them staring. I could almost sense a lustful spirit in their fixed gaze. I wanted to give them a good sermon on 'respecting women'. Usually I did give a sermon on 'modesty' to my girls . . . just to remind them.

~~~

God gave a desire for intimacy and sexual fulfilment to be satisfied in the privacy of marriage. When a man vows to 'forsake all others' it also means to forsake looking at and thinking about them. Jesus taught that adultery of the heart can occur by looking on a woman with desire for her. It may seem innocent enough to 'look' at other women and 'admire' their beauty. But if most men were honest with themselves, they would admit that it doesn't stop there. It's time to face up to the fact that it's lust. Keeping in shape is a healthy habit, but it can become an obsession fed by pride.

There's nothing wrong with looking good. It's the motivation of one's heart that God is concerned with. Faithfulness in marriage makes the relationship special and unique. The wife gives herself (her desires as well as her body) only to her husband. The husband gives himself (his thoughts as well as his actions) only to his wife. This exclusivity builds a strong bond between the two and truly makes them one in spirit.
~~~

Pornography is a gross betrayal of the trust and purity in the marriage relationship. The sex-sellers are everywhere. If you cannot monitor the internet, television, movie-viewing, magazines or the beach, you may need to eliminate them. But you'll still have to deal with the spiritual issue that lies behind your behavior. God has a wonderful plan for man and his sexuality. It is only when a man allows the Holy Spirit to convict him of impure motives and desires within his heart that he can be healed and experience the fulfillment God has for him.

Temptation is everywhere. Someone once said, "just because it's there doesn't mean you have to take it." That's so true when it comes to being faithful to the vow to 'forsake all others'. We all have to make decisions for ourselves. Very seldom are we *forced* into situations that lead to violating our wedding vows. We need to be on our guard to recognize temptation and resist. It means putting your spouse first, before anyone and anything else. It involves becoming best friends with each other. Faithfulness to that vow is developed through honesty, self-control, sensitivity, agape love, understanding, patience and gentleness. Married love, seasoned by shared intimacy and spiritual maturity, becomes richer and more fulfilling.

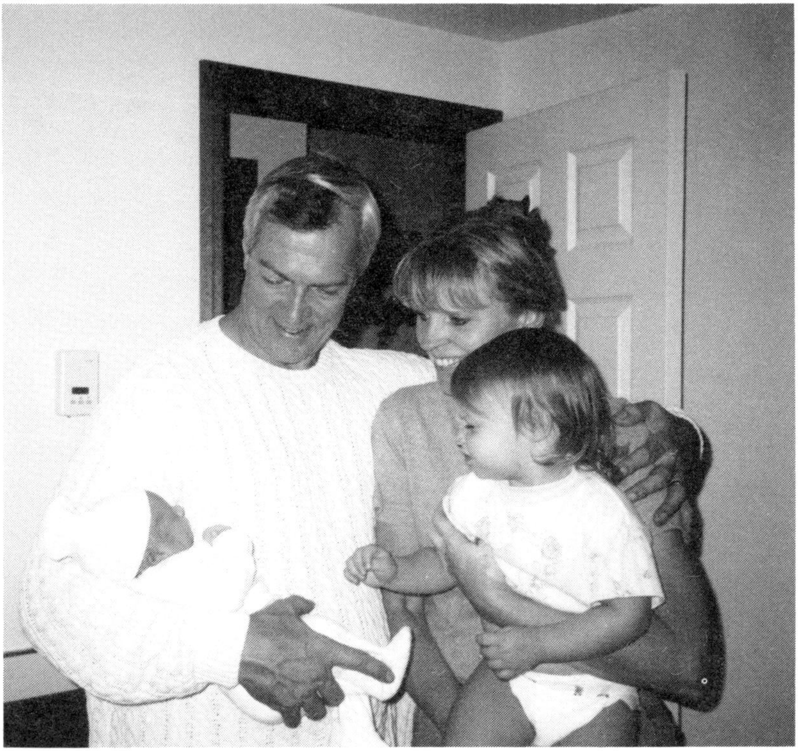

Chapter 6

As long as you both shall live

I remember standing at the altar contemplating this phrase thinking . . .

We have our entire lives ahead of us. People really don't start going down hill until they're at least in their mid-thirties. Dad and Mom are in their late forties and they still have loads of fun. But I can't imagine us ever being forty-five. Of course, Cheri's mom is about that age and she looks great. Dad always told me, "Take a good look at the girl's mother because that's pretty much the way she'll look in twenty years." Of course as Cheri grows older, so will I. There sits Cheri's two grandmothers. They're great old gals. Someday Cheri will be a grandmother. And I guess that would make me a grandfather. Well, that's a long way off. No use thinking about things like that. We have a great life ahead of us, We're young, full of energy and ambition. Everything's perfect!

~~~

Twenty-five years later I was wondering where all the time had gone. I really wanted to finish videotaping the song I had written for our second daughter Kimberly before her new baby arrived. Where had all the years gone? That old saying *'the older you get*
~~~

the quicker time goes by' sure is true. To think that we were going to be grandparents again was incredible. How could that possibly be? I could close my eyes and be twenty-one again. I still felt that young. I remember Cheri with her long, straight, blonde hair, and those bell-bottom, corduroy slacks. It seemed like yesterday when Kimberly was born, and now, *she's* having her *second* baby. I knew the song was a little corny, but Kim would appreciate its sentiments.

I thought girls were just for fun,
Never got serious with anyone;
Then came my baby and a change you'd see,
I was saying,"Will you marry me?"

It didn't take long 'til we were altar bound,
A greater love could not be found;
Our love grew and then she came to me,
"Hey Honey, we're having a baby."

My baby's havin' a baby,
It's for sure and I don't mean maybe;
I'm gonna be a daddy, what should I do?
Hey baby, I love you.

The next nine months that little life grew,
A girl or a boy we hadn't a clue;
Then came the greatest moment in my life,
A little girl's born from the love of my wife.

My baby's havin' a baby
It's for sure and I don't mean maybe;
I'm gonna be a daddy, lot's to do;
Hey baby, I love you.

She grew up strong -- brought us so much joy
Time flew by, now who's that boy?
My baby was married; soon she phoned me,
"Hi Grandpa, we're havin' a baby."

My baby's havin' a baby
It's for sure and I don't mean maybe;
I'm a Grandpa and I know what to do,
Hey baby, I'll love you.

~~~

It was about that time I had a little difficulty with the aging process. Don't get me wrong, I knew that each stage of life had its benefits. The early years of marriage were loads of fun as we were so young and impulsive. We had so much energy that material things just didn't matter too much. I remember how we would watch for 'furniture bargains' by the curbside on garbage day. We were masters at turning someone's trash into our treasure. The table we made out of a wire spool was ingenious, at least we thought so. Making ends meet became an adventure. We could be arguing one minute and in a passionate embrace the next. The excitement of having children and raising a
~~~

family was challenging but fulfilling. I remember how I would skip lunch and race home to listen to Rochelle's first words and try to teach her a few new ones. The school activities, sports, plays, and concerts kept us running. That time in our life was so rewarding. Watching the girls fall in love, replacing me as the number one man in their lives, was a painful but joyous experience. Then we entered the empty nest stage; now ***that*** was a time of mixed emotions. After twenty-three years of kids in the house we were back to just the two of us. It was devastating for a few days. It's funny to even think back on it now. All that mourning and then the revelation of our new found freedom. We didn't have to deal with so many personalities, schedules and opinions all the time. We could snuggle together on the couch without the threat of someone walking in and I could walk around the house in my underwear again! Then we had the joy of becoming grandparents. The bumper sticker says it best, "If I knew grand kids were going to be so much fun, I would have had them first."

But I wasn't dealing quite so well with other aspects of aging. Why was my hair getting so grey and thin? What's the deal about losing hair where you want it and growing hair where you never had it before? Cheri had aged so gracefully. I still thought she was the most beautiful woman in the world. No matter how the years had changed us, I loved her more than I ever had before. Still, I wondered if I might be experiencing a 'mid-life crisis'; I was experiencing so much frustration. Then I heard a familiar voice ministering to me, just as if He understood my feelings without me having to utter a word . . .

Scott, life is a series of stages. Each is filled with challenge and reward. Youth lacks wisdom, but has energy. Maturity brings with it understanding and stability. Life is made up of birth, aging and death. The fulfillment derived from observing the fruit of a life's labors can not be equaled by any other stage. Don't struggle with this process. Enjoy each moment. You'll never pass this way again.

~~~

Cheri and I had both aged. Although it had been a graceful process, there was no hiding that the years had an effect on us. As a pastor I was well aware of the struggle many men had with this. Often, in a desire to hang on to youth, men would leave their life-long helpmate, thinking that a younger woman would make them feel younger. The irony is that without God's blessing, they still didn't find fulfillment in their lives. God honors faithfulness. He is a covenant God. He wants men of commitment. He despises the betrayal of the marriage covenant.

A major issue that can arise in a marriage after many years is that of comparison. Because of his own insecurity with his appearance, a man might mistakenly
~~~

assume that if a younger woman finds him attractive he will feel younger; he will have a better self-image. He compares his 'older' wife to the younger woman. He sees his wife's imperfections and thinks that if he was accompanied by a younger woman he would also look and act younger. But, breaking the marriage covenant won't solve his problem. His problem is not his wife . . . it's himself. Instead of despising the inevitable -- that he's getting older -- he needs to enjoy this stage of maturity and refinement. He needs to see the rewards of the experiences of a lifetime.

Soldiers proudly wear badges and medals as reminders of their heroism and accomplishments. Mature men and women need to view wrinkles as badges of honor, representing years of smiling and filling the home with joy. Some of those creases in the brow reflect prayers and concern for a sick child or a teen that stayed out too late. Weather-beaten hands show the signs of thousands of hours in water, washing dishes, doing laundry, and cleaning the house. Spider and varicose veins, even stretch marks are medals for a mother's gift of life to a child. They reveal the sacrifice of countless hours walking the floors with a child in her arms.

Everyone grows older each day he is alive. Your attitude is more important than your age. Growing old is a beautiful gift that deserves honor and respect.

~~~
~~~

Cheri and I have started working out together at the Y.M.C.A. and have tried to be less critical of ourselves and our changes in appearance. Eating better and our regiment of taking vitamins has definitely increased our energy levels. Beyond the physical, the Lord is helping us to appreciate this special time of our lives. As far as Cheri is concerned, I value her like a fine wine; she keeps getting better with time. The titles 'Grandpa and Grandma' are precious to us and we wear them proudly. Cheri even has one of those necklaces with all the little birthstone kids on it. She has our own three children, the girls' husbands and all the grand kids represented; she even has a little angel for our granddaughter Rebecca who is safe in the arms of Jesus. Cheri says that she's chosen to enjoy the fact that we're both looking a little older. We're old enough to look like we have some wisdom and experience to offer, and young enough for people to be surprised that we have four grandchildren.

CHAPS

Chapter 7

If so, answer "I do."

The pastor was looking directly at me. I glanced at Cheri and began to analyze . . .

This is the queen-mother of all vows. Should I take a little more time to think this one over? I wonder if anyone has ever come to this point and said "No, I'm not going to do it." Am I really sure? This probably isn't the time to be asking questions like this. There stand my groomsmen, all single. What will they do without me? I'm breaking up the old gang. They were shocked when I announced I was getting married. They've spent the past few months trying to talk me out of it. If there's one thing that my dad taught me it was to keep commitments. When you say yes to something, that's it, it's settled. Anytime we talked about joining a team or considered a new job, Dad would always tell us, "Think it through. If you're going to start it I expect you to see it through." With few exceptions, no matter how bad the situation became, we never quit. I've thought about this for months. This is what I want. Cheri is God's choice for me. I can make this vow. Yes, I can and I want to. ***"I do!"***

~~~
~~~

Approximately twenty years into our marriage I wondered if the word 'commitment' meant anything to anyone besides me. My whole life had been committed to helping others. Sometimes I was convinced that nobody cared. It seemed like no one appreciated anything I did. I slaved away sixty to eighty hours a week, helping people with their problems, praying for them, but did they care? I was so engrossed in self-pity that I was certain that no amount of money, time spent, or niceties could please Cheri. Nothing I ever said or did seemed to be right. Then to top it off, a business partner who was one of my best friends stabbed me in the back. It just didn't seem worth it. I remember reasoning that if Cheri's so miserable *with* me, maybe I should do one last good deed and leave her. No one to leave a mess, no one to clean up after, no socks to turn right-side-out. She deserved some happiness and she sure didn't seem to be finding it with me. I thought about getting on my boat and heading for an island. It wasn't just Cheri, it was people in general. I wanted to do something for *me* for a change. I considered that perhaps I wasn't cut out for this vocation. It was a real good time to call out to God . . .

Hey God, are you still listening to me? I think I'm in trouble here. The fact is, I know I am. I'm becoming just like all those non-committed people I've criticized. You know that I've always been an 'I do' kind of guy. But lately, I find myself feeling like it's 'I can't', 'I won't' or 'I don't want to'.

(God speaks . . .) *Scott, do you remember the day when a man's word was his pledge? When a person said 'I do' it didn't mean 'I might' or 'I'll see how things go'. It meant 'the thing I promise will definitely be accomplished, no questions asked'. The 'I will' or 'I do' of marriage is the most important commitment a man could ever make. I heard you make that vow as did all of heaven, a church full of people, and your whole family. Your 'I do' was forever. I never promised that it would be easy, but I* ***did*** *promise to help you with it. Don't allow the pressures of your job to shake you. The covenant you made with Cheri needs to remain your primary focus.*

~~~

Cheri and I have found that it's important to view marriage as a covenant rather than a contract. A **contract** is an agreement between parties based upon certain conditions and considerations and may be voided if those conditions and considerations are not carried out. The contract has limited liability and is based on distrust. A **covenant** has unlimited responsibility and is based on trust. The marriage covenant is a sacred trust. No other covenant can cause as much damage when broken. Together we have witnessed the untold pain and suffering of many
~~~

who have broken their vows. Throughout the Old Testament there are stories about those with whom God made covenant. Those who kept the covenants were ultimately blessed. In Genesis nine verse nine God spoke to Noah and said that the covenant was between Noah and his descendants, an eternal covenant. God told Abraham that the covenant he was making with him was for all generations, an everlasting covenant. The covenants that God made with these men were sealed with animal sacrifices. The killing and letting of blood was a grim reminder of the seriousness of the covenant. Blood was the life of the animal. No blood -- no life. Covenant was the lifeblood of the relationship God had with these men. With the introduction of circumcision, man carried an actual mark or symbol on his body, a memorial of covenant. He was constantly reminded of the covenant he had made. In His infinite wisdom God chose the male sex organ to carry this memorial because of its role in propagation. The covenants you make, whether good or bad, will affect your offspring -- either positively or adversely.

In Malachi chapter two we read the dialog between God and the prophet. God was upset with the children of Israel. He was very quick to respond to the inquiry made as to the reason for His displeasure. The bottom line was that the men were not honoring their covenant with their wives. They were divorcing and committing adultery. God asked, *"Did I not make you one?" "How do you expect to have Godly seed?"* God threatened to cut them off, denying them salvation, if they continued in this sin.

Just as circumcision was a reminder of the covenant between Abraham and God, the wedding ring is the symbol of the marriage covenant. When we look at our wedding bands we see a reminder of the covenant we made. To other men and women it says, "Hands off. I belong to someone."

The marriage covenant is a most sacred covenant. The covenant you made with your wife is the glue that can hold everything together when all else fails. Eliminate the option of breaking your word. Some options are not available to a man of God. Breaking the marriage covenant is one of them. Don't let the thought of divorce **ever** be an option. Faithfulness in marriage is obedience to God.

~~~

On our twenty-fifth anniversary we had a wedding ceremony and renewed our wedding vows. There were tears as we looked into each other's eyes. It wasn't the twinkle of youthful infatuation, but that of a mature love, developed through the years, based on faith and faithfulness. There's no longer any question about the **'I do'.**
~~~

THE FINAL WORD

Outside of salvation, the most wonderful gift God gives you is your wife. She is a precious gift from God and needs to be treated as such. Like never before in our country's history, men are succumbing to the world's pressures and are becoming covenant breakers. The Marines have always boasted of the toughness of their men. God is looking for a few good men in this final chapter of history who will rise up above the world and be promise keepers, men of covenant. The Word of God shows us that keeping one's word is the mark of a real man. Avoid the traps that the enemy lays before you: pornography, fantasy, substance abuse, gambling, workaholism, over-indulgence with sports or hobbies. Make sure your sexual relationship with your wife is based on love -- not lust. Put God first in your life followed by your wife as a close second. Spend time making sure that your relationship with God and your wife is where it needs to be. Be active in a church; have prayer and devotions with your family.

Most men have within them a desire to win. Whether it's on the athletic field or in the business place, there is an innate desire to succeed and prove oneself. The wise man finds out early that in the game of life there are only two challenges that really count. Neither depends upon a man's size, physical ability, education or IQ. We are talking about developing your relationships with God and your wife. All men start with the same opportunity to succeed. You ***can*** win in these most important of life's games. It's never too late to start: start today! "Be all that you can be." Join the ranks of the many men who have chosen to remain faithful to their marriage vows.

A current catalogue of books
written by Scott ♥ Cheri Scheer
is available online at

www.familyministries.net

Scott ♥ Cheri Scheer